Top DOgs

I Love My
Pug

Abigail Beal

PowerKiDS
press
New York

This book is dedicated to you and your pet— a special friendship based on loyalty, respect, and kindness.

Published in 2011 by The Rosen Publishing Group, Inc.
29 East 21st Street, New York, NY 10010

First Edition

Editor: Joanne Randolph
Book Design: Greg Tucker

Photo Credits: Cover, pp. 4, 8, 9, 11, 12–13, 16–17, 20 (left), 20–21, 22 Shutterstock.com; p. 5 Ryan McVay/Digital Vision/Thinkstock; p. 6 Louis Michel van Loo/Getty Images; p. 7 Buyenlarge/Getty Images; p. 10 Mark Raycroft/Getty Images; p. 14 (inset) Digital Vision/Photodisc/Thinkstock; pp. 14–15 Emily Keegin/Getty Images; p. 15 (right) Ariel Skelley/Getty Images; p. 18 © Juniors Bildarchiv/age fotostock; p. 19 Jupiterimages/Polka Dot/Thinkstock.

Library of Congress Cataloging-in-Publication Data

Beal, Abigail.
I love my pug / by Abigail Beal. — 1st ed.
    p. cm. — (Top dogs)
Includes index.
ISBN 978-1-4488-2539-4 (library binding) — ISBN 978-1-4488-2662-9 (pbk.) —
ISBN 978-1-4488-2663-6 (6-pack)
1. Pug—Juvenile literature. I. Title.
SF429.P9B43 2011
636.76—dc22
                    2010025766

Manufactured in the United States of America

CPSIA Compliance Information: Batch #WW11PK: For Further Information contact Rosen Publishing, New York, New York at 1-800-237-9932

Contents

Meet the Pug

One look in a pug's eyes tells you everything you need to know. This small **breed** is known for being friendly and playful. Once bred for Chinese **royalty**, pugs today make great family pets.

Pugs have lots of **personality**. Many people pick them because they have great

Pugs have round faces and short noses. They often have black fur around their noses and mouths and on their ears.

4

charm. Pugs are smart dogs that want to please their owners. This can make some pugs easy to train. However, pugs are known for being **stubborn**, too. Luckily this breed is also known for being loving and outgoing. Are you ready to find out more about pugs?

Pugs are small enough to pick up but sturdy enough to be around children.

Pug History

Pugs were first bred in China. The Happa dog was likely used to help make the breed. The Happa dog was a small, short-haired dog that also helped make the Pekingese breed. Pugs are believed to have lived in China as early as 1115 BC. No record of them is available until 663 BC, though. Ruling classes or

Princess Ekaterina Golitsyna, of Russia, is pictured with her pug in 1757.

members of the royal court often owned pugs. These dogs were so prized that they had their own servants and titles!

The pug became well liked throughout Europe because many kings and queens owned this breed. Pugs were brought to North America in the 1800s.

Here a young boy sits with his two pugs in the 1900s in the United States.

A Face You'll Never Forget

Here you can see this pug's wrinkled head. You can also see the curled tail that sits on top of its back.

Once you have seen a pug, you will never forget how it looks. Pugs are known for their round, wrinkled heads. Their **muzzles** are quite short, too.

A pug is a toy breed, which means it is a small dog. Pugs are real dogs, though! They are known for being strong despite

The Latin word *pugnus* means "fist" and may be where the pug's name comes from. It is thought that a pug's face looks like a tightly closed fist.

their short, stocky bodies. Their short coats are silver, apricot, or black and are soft and shiny. A pug's ears are small and soft. Its tail curls up over its body.

Popular Pugs

The pug is a popular, or well-liked, pet. Many people pick pugs for their small size. Adult pugs weigh between 14 and 18 pounds (6–8 kg). People also pick this breed because pugs are funny and friendly dogs. This dog is also very clean.

The pug is quite **loyal** and will try to keep its owner safe.

Pugs can make great friends for other dogs, large or small. It is important to let them meet other dogs at a young age, though.

Pugs are known for a bark that is far bigger than they are! They are very **devoted** to their owners. They want to be with their people and to please them. Playful pugs are wonderful pets for children. While some small dogs can be easily hurt, pugs are strong. They are always ready to have fun, too.

Pugs love their families and are good dogs for families with children. They are great for grown-ups, too, though!

Friendly and Hungry

Pugs are even tempered dogs that get along with older people, children, and other dogs. Just like any dog, though, your pug should be **socialized** at a young age. This means you should introduce your puppy to new people, places, and things. This will help it feel comfortable in new situations.

Pugs are not just known for being friendly. They are also known for enjoying their food. Pug owners need to be careful not to give their dogs too much food or too many treats. Pugs are small, but they still need exercise. Walks and active play will help them stay at a healthy weight.

Pugs need exercise to stay healthy. Running, walking, and playing are all easy and fun ways to exercise your pet.

Caring for Your Pug

Pug owners want their pets to live long, healthy lives. Taking good care of your pet is one way to make sure this happens. Feeding your dog good food and giving it clean water is important.

Pugs are small enough to be bathed in sinks or bathtubs. They can also be bathed outside.

Pugs need to visit the vet yearly. The vet will give your pet a checkup and make sure it is up to date on its shots.

Pugs have short fur, so they do not need to be brushed that often. However, you will need to bathe your dog every so often. Energetic, strong pugs need exercise every day. All dogs need to see a veterinarian at least once a year and more often if they are sick.

Be sure to put a collar on your pug with a tag that has your name and phone number on it.

Things to Watch Out For

Every dog breed has its own special health **concerns**. If you get a dog from a good breeder, you will have fewer problems. It is still important to know what to watch out for, though. You want to help your dog stay healthy!

Pugs have lots of wrinkles on their faces. These wrinkles are part of what gives them their charm! However, the wrinkles need to be kept clean so your pug does not get skin **infections**. Pugs have short muzzles. This means the passages inside their noses are shorter, too. This can make it hard for pugs to breathe. They also have trouble cooling their bodies down on hot days.

Be gentle when you check or clean your pug's wrinkles. You do not want to hurt its skin.

Stay, Pug!

By training your pug, you teach it how to act around others. You are also teaching it how you want it to **respond** to commands, such as *sit*, *stay*, and *down*.

Training begins when your dog is just a puppy. You will teach it how to act around family members and other dogs.

This pug is being taught to sit. The basic commands that you teach your pet can be building blocks for harder tricks.

The most important tools for training any dog are **consistency** and **praise**. Praise your pug when it does what you ask. Early in training, a small treat can be given to **reinforce** a new skill. Remember that pugs often eat too much, though. Try to use other rewards, too.

Teach your pug to heel, or walk by your side. A pug that pulls at the end of its leash is not as much fun to walk.

Why Pick a Pug?

There are many reasons to pick a pug. Pugs are smart. They are very loving and loyal to their owners, too. Pugs can be a good pick if a person lives in an apartment or does not have a large yard. This does not mean your pug never needs to go outside or take walks, though. Pugs need exercise, as any dog does.

Pugs are cute, playful dogs. Are they the right dog for you?

People who own pugs will tell you that there is not a better dog breed out there. If you love your pug, then it is sure to love you back!

Pug Facts

1. A breed **standard** for the pug was made following the start of the Pug Dog Club of Britain in 1883. That breed standard is the same today.

2. Pugs can catch colds easily.

3. The pug was most popular during the Victorian era, which lasted from 1837 to 1901 while Queen Victoria ruled England.

4. A pug can be rose eared or button eared. The button-eared pugs are considered the breed standard.

5. Lady Brassy from England made black pugs popular when she brought a pair back from China for a dog show in the 1870s.

6. Napoléon Bonaparte's wife Joséphine de Beauharnais had a pug named Fortune. Josephine and her husband used the pug to send secret messages to each other.

7. Many famous people today own pugs, too. Billy Joel owns a pug named Fionula. Jessica Alba owns pugs named Sid and Nancy, and Dennis Quaid owns a pug named Pudgy.

Glossary

breed (BREED) A group of animals that look alike and have the same relatives.

charm (CHAHRM) Ease at winning people's hearts.

concerns (kun-SERNZ) Worries or problems.

consistency (kun-SIS-ten-see) Staying the same.

devoted (dih-VOHT-ed) Gave effort, attention, and time to a purpose.

infections (in-FEK-shunz) Sicknesses caused by germs.

loyal (LOY-ul) Faithful to a person or an idea.

muzzles (MUH-zelz) Parts of animals' heads that come forward and include their noses.

personality (per-sun-A-lih-tee) How a person or an animal acts with others.

praise (PRAYZ) Saying nice things about someone or something.

reinforce (ree-in-FORS) To strengthen.

respond (rih-SPOND) To answer.

royalty (ROY-ul-tee) Kings, queens, and their families.

socialized (SOH-shuh-lyzd) Made ready to be around others.

standard (STAN-derd) A rule used to set an example.

stubborn (STUH-burn) Wanting to have one's own way.

Index

Web Sites

Due to the changing nature of Internet links, PowerKids Press has developed an online list of Web sites related to the subject of this book. This site is updated regularly. Please use this link to access the list:
www.powerkidslinks.com/topd/pug/

24